marzipan

This book is dedicated to Guido Jans, whose original idea this was and who designed and produced these delightful marzipan figures. Sadly, he did not live to see the results of his work.

marzipan

AUTHOR
Guido Jans

PHOTOGRAPHY
Michel De Meyer

FALL
RIVER
PRESS

Preface

My aim in this book is to introduce you to a variety of techniques and options for making marzipan figures in a simple and contemporary way—handmade but well thought out and stylishly conceived. Whether you are a dextrous amateur wanting to make a marzipan model for a special occasion, or a professional confectioner looking for guidance and inspiration, this book is for you.

The first thing to stress is the importance of working with genuine, good-quality marzipan. Really top-quality commercially made marzipan is widely available. Look for a brand made by the Lübecker method—this uses lightly toasted almonds, which add an exceptionally good flavor to the marzipan. This is the quality that I use. It has at least 60 percent sugar and up to 40 percent almonds with added invertin, which helps it stay soft for longer. The 50 percent variety is more troublesome and too soft to mold into figures.

If you want to make your own marzipan, there are dozens of recipes in specialty magazines or on the Internet, or try the recipes found on page 12. Making a small quantity of marzipan is no problem for the amateur—for making larger quantities, it is useful to have specialty equipment such as a rolling machine. Preservation is also quite a challenge: temperature, light, and hygiene are just some of the factors to keep in mind.

You don't need to be an artistic genius in order to make marzipan models. You will find that some designs and ideas involve a little more intricate work than others, but don't give up at the first attempt. Just give your imagination free rein and do your best. There's no need to try to reproduce the figures identically: we all have our own creative approach and way of expressing ourselves.

TIPS FOR MAKING A SUCCESSFUL MARZIPAN MODEL

- You need to ensure that everything is firmly attached to prevent pieces breaking off when shaping the figure or when packaging it. Attach each part as quickly as possible before the base dries. You can secure them afterward using syrup, egg white, melted chocolate, apricot jam, or cocoa butter.
- To stop your masterpieces from drying out, apply warm cocoa butter (heat to 131°F) with an atomizer or paintbrush. Otherwise, use a quality gloss based on gum arabic.
- Use food coloring to make the figures look both appetizing and appealing. Try introducing a few comic touches, such as exaggeratedly thick, red lips, but don't overdo it: too much detail can spoil the effect.
- Always accentuate the figure's cheeks using an airbrush and food coloring.
- The most important part of a figure's face is, of course, the eyes—so take time to get them right. The expression needs to communicate. With that in mind, do not make the egg-white frosting too thick or too thin—you need a smooth finish. Position the black pupils precisely so that they both look in the same direction. And do not make them too small.
- Creating black coloring is quite tricky and the degree of color achieved also depends on the type and base color of the marzipan you are using. Experiment with equal, small amounts of blue, yellow, and red coloring, adding a little more red if the black is not dense enough. Alternatively, there are a number of commercial companies selling black food coloring on the Internet. You could also use chocolate but it will not produce a true black.

Professional confectioners keen to produce larger quantities of marzipan figures should also bear the following in mind:

- Working conditions can cause problems. It is advisable to use a workspace that has been hygienically prepared and preferably one that is used exclusively for working marzipan. It is a good idea to wear latex gloves if your hands are becoming clammy—marzipan is a sticky substance.
- Make sure you are working in a comfortable position.
- Avoid working the marzipan for too long—this will alter its consistency, and it will start to exude oil and look unappealing.
- To make cost-effective figures, produce 50 or so heads and bodies in one go. This will prevent your work from becoming too monotonous, while allowing you to achieve the end result within a reasonable period of time.

Guido Jans

INTRODUCTION

I am proud to have been asked by my friend Guido to write a few words of introduction to this book, which is beautiful, useful, amusing, and practical.

Guido's great predilection for marzipan was well-known throughout the Netherlands, Japan, France, Germany, and many other countries. The professional pride and expertise embodied by Guido Jans are evident in his concise use of language. His enthusiasm was always inspirational, and throughout this book he gives amateurs and professionals alike the chance to aim for excellence when modeling with marzipan. And simply leafing through the book is an entertainment in itself.

This book contains a wealth of hints and ideas for today's enthusiastic, high-tempo confectioners. As an artist, Guido took a whimsical, comical, or affectionate approach toward the designs and figures he used to create these delightful confections.

Marzipan is a definitive guide to marzipan, a beautiful gift, and a tribute to Guido's work. The photographic illustrations of his methods will assist your modeling and make it a pleasure.

This splendid volume about marzipan will be an enjoyable page-turner, dear Guido. It is a fine reflection of the inspiring person you were and whom we all miss. I should like to offer you both my congratulations and my heartfelt thanks.

Paul Provoost
Chairman of Richemont Seniors Belgium
Honorary Chairman of the International Richemont Club

A SOURCE OF INSPIRATION

I take pleasure in recommending Guido Jans' marzipan figures to you all—consumers and professional colleagues alike.

As the technical advisor to the association of the best confectioners in the Netherlands, I became acquainted a number of years ago with the special and distinctive style of Guido's work.

Most importantly, marzipan is a delicious treat made from pure almonds with just enough sugar to turn it into a mouth-watering item of confectionery. Yet marzipan also gives bakers and confectioners the opportunity to indulge themselves in terms of design and current trends. The style and techniques that Guido applied to his marzipan creations were quite exceptional because of their cunning simplicity. The figures that he produced for this book are strikingly expressive, sometimes with a wonderful air of mischief about them. They are instantly cheerful, move us to laughter, and, as a result, have brought a very welcome extra dimension to marzipan.

When creating edible designs, it is important to pay attention to the material you are using, in this case, marzipan—you cannot, for example, model marzipan as you would clay. With a delicate touch, you can be as creative as you like but still produce something that tastes every bit as good as it looks. The techniques demonstrated in this book will teach young professional confectioners (and keen amateurs) how to use their equipment and resources correctly, and ensure that working with marzipan soon becomes great fun. They challenge us to give free rein to our creative ideas.

The figures created by Guido Jans have always been a joy to behold—they are a pleasure to receive as a gift and to enjoy eating. This book is a highly practical addition to any cookbook collection and will be a source of inspiration and enjoyment for all its readers.

Peter de Wit
Technical Advisor for Heerlijk & Heerlijk in the Netherlands
Colleague and friend of Guido Jans

Contents

Marzipan 101

For centuries, marzipan has been used
as a medium for decorating food.
The two constants when preparing
marzipan are almonds and sugar.
But you introduce variety by adding
colors and/or flavorings, coming
up with new designs, and
incorporating accessories.

History

Marzipan is believed to have originated in Mesopotamia, the ancient land between the Tigris and Euphrates rivers in the Middle East. It is most likely that honey was originally used together with finely ground almonds to create a pliable paste.

It was at the time of the Crusades that Europeans first discovered marzipan—and fell in love with it. By then, the Moors on the Iberian Peninsula had already introduced marzipan as a greatly coveted and expensive confection, since sugar and almonds were costly ingredients. In the Middle Ages, marzipan was made using cane sugar, which could only be purchased from an apothecary. Because of the colorings and flavorings added to it, marzipan was hailed for its medicinal properties—more often than not, erroneously—and it sold for a fortune.

Gradual growth in sugar production over the centuries undoubtedly contributed toward marzipan's steady rise in popularity and affordability.

This exceptional confection has long been a favorite accompaniment to festive occasions. Leonardo da Vinci used it to create ephemeral works of art that adorned the tables of royalty and the wealthy. To this day, almost any event in our lives can be illustrated through this highly malleable medium. Almost all of us will have some happy memory or association with marzipan: a childhood Christmas, a birthday cake, celebrations among friends and family, or simply gazing longingly at the baker's window display…

Recipes

You can buy marzipan ready-made from specialty confectionery or cake-decorating stores or from a supermarket cake-baking section. This is made under professional conditions and is ideal to work with.

If you want to make your own marzipan, try the recipes below.

UNCOOKED RECIPE
2 lb blanched almonds
2 lb white granulated sugar
2 lb confectioners' sugar without starch to prevent fermentation
½ teaspoon orange blossom water

Mix the almonds and the sugar together, and finely grind in a food processor.
Knead to a smooth paste, gradually adding small amounts of confectioners' sugar as you go.
Finally, add the orange blossom water, and knead in thoroughly.

Note:
You can also make marzipan using ground almonds.

Use the same quantities, but add 2 egg whites to the mixture.
Keep kneading until you get a smooth, even dough.

COOKED RECIPE
4 lb sugar
7 oz glucose
2 lb blanched almonds
1¼ lb confectioners' sugar

Pour ¼ of the sugar and the glucose into ¾ cup water and heat to no less than 245°F and no more than 257°F. The warmer the sugar–glucose preparation, the more robust the marzipan will be.
Grind up the almonds with the rest of the sugar.
Gradually drizzle the dissolved sugar and glucose over the ground almond/sugar mixture, adding small amounts of confectioners' sugar as you go and stirring until it becomes a smooth paste.

Coloring

Colored marzipan allows you to create an even more attractive and realistic model. You can either color the marzipan paste before modeling or "paint" the model.

To color the paste before you start modeling, add food coloring a little at a time and knead it thoroughly before adding more—this will enable you to keep a check on how it affects the overall color. To color modeled marzipan, it is best to use an airbrush. In both cases, always remember to build up the color gradually and never add too much color in one go.

Dividing

Professional confectioners use special tools and graduated rules to measure off equal quantities of marzipan. These devices are particularly useful if you want to produce a large batch of identical models.

If you are an amateur confectioner, bear in mind that it is more difficult to create a large model than a smaller one—you need greater expertise and experience to keep a large mass of material balanced and harmonious.

Basic shapes

BALL
Roll the amount of marzipan you need between both hands to create a smooth ball. Keep your hands as flat as possible when doing this.

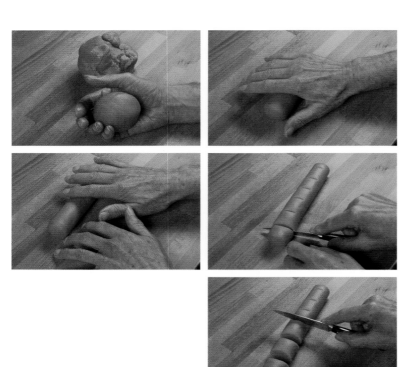

STICK
Roll out the amount you need on a smooth surface using the flat of one hand. Increase the pressure to lengthen the stick.

Use a flat piece of wood to create a longer, more uniformly molded stick.

BULB SHAPE
Start off with a smooth ball, roll using the edge of both palms, and create the tapered end to the bulb by applying gentle pressure toward the wrists.

PEAR SHAPE
Start off with a smooth ball.
Squeeze the marzipan into a pear shape by applying gentle pressure between the base of the palms and the wrists.

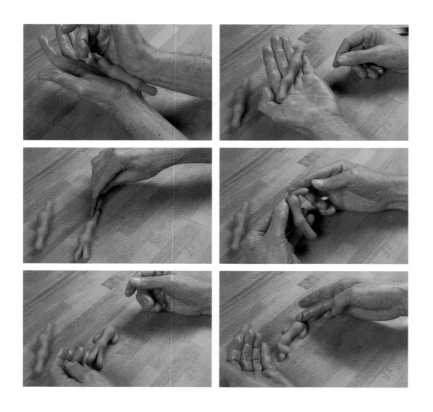

BODIES

Simple body

First create a pear shape from a smooth ball of marzipan.

Turn the pear shape around, and create the same shape at the other end.

Using a sharp knife, bisect the two ends.

Now model the body to create either a sitting or lying figure.

Straddling the legs will make the finished model more stable.

Anatomical body

Start off with a smooth ball, and gently
press the marzipan between the base
of the palms and the wrists to create
a pear shape.

Give the shape a quarter turn and push
out a second limb toward you.

Turn the figure around and repeat to
create two more limbs.

Now model the body to create either
a sitting or lying figure.

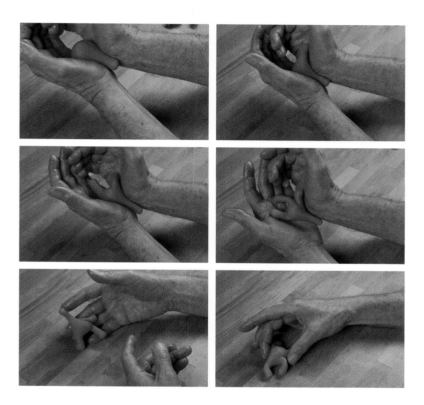

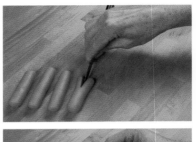

Using a stick as a body

Use a flat piece of wood to create an even stick.
Use scissors or a knife to bisect both ends, and then create either a standing or lying figure.

Sitting body

Start off with a smooth ball, and gently press the marzipan into a pear shape. Cut into the bulbous sides using a sharp knife to create the line of the legs.

HEADS

Dog

Start off with a smooth ball, and gently
press the marzipan into a pear shape.
Give the figure a quarter turn, and create
another taper.
Roll the middle section into a point, and
pinch the ears gently into shape between
your thumb and forefinger.
Carefully attach the head to the body.
Create the eyes using the point of a
knife, and complete the nose with a tiny
ball of marzipan.

Note: You can use small amounts of syrup,
egg white, cocoa butter, melted chocolate,
or apricot jam to attach the head, hands,
hair, etc., firmly to the main body, or to
keep the figure upright on a base. In some
projects we have used toothpicks or dry
spaghetti to secure the components. Do
ensure these inedible parts are removed
before the treats are eaten.

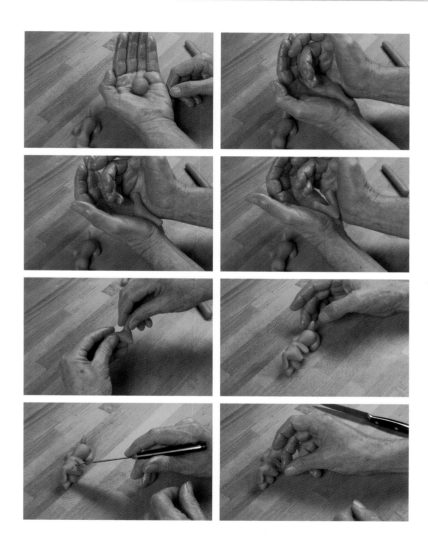

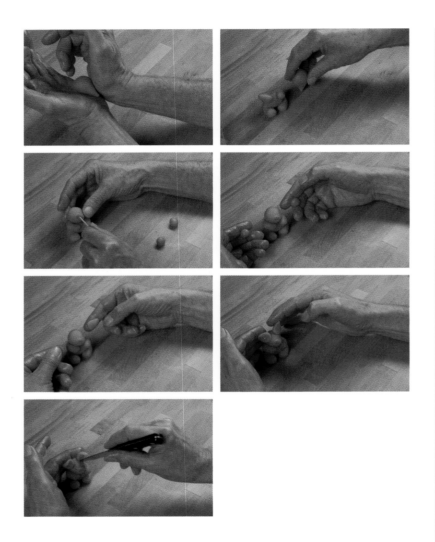

Pig

Start off with a pointed pear shape, and gently press the snout flat on the work surface.

Attach the head to the body.

Prick out the nostrils using a toothpick.

For the ears, flatten two small balls of marzipan between your thumb and forefinger. Fix them to the head, folding them slightly forward.

Cut the eyes using the point of a sharp knife.

Cat or fox

Start off with a smooth ball, and create
a pointed, but short, pear shape.
Give the figure a quarter turn and form
the ears. Shape the middle section into
a point, and add the eyes using the point
of a knife.
Fix the head to the body.

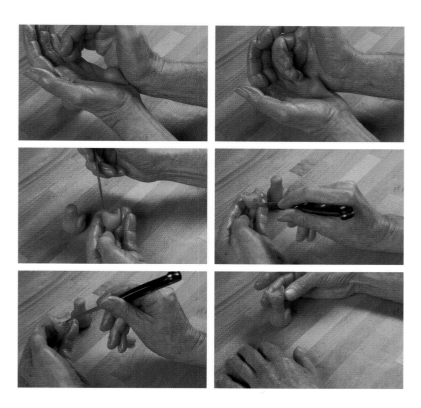

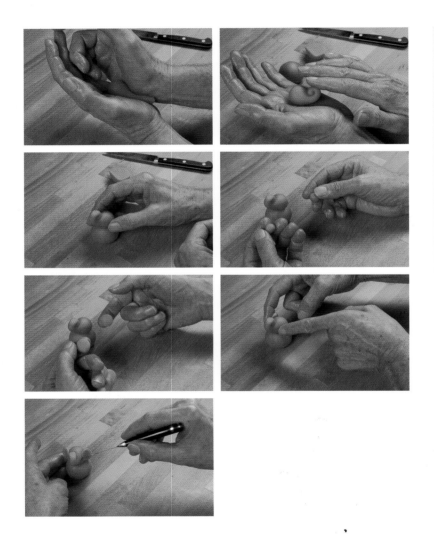

Elephant

Start off with a smooth ball, and create a pointed, extended pear shape.
Roll up the trunk.
Flatten two small, smooth balls of marzipan between your thumb and forefinger, and attach these to the head. Mark the eyes using the point of a knife.

TULIP

You will need two bulb-shaped balls for each tulip.

Cut crossways into the bulb you are using for the flower, and make just one incision in the bulb for the leaves.

Attach the flower to the leaves with a piece of dry spaghetti or a toothpick.

Note: Do ensure dry spaghetti is removed before the tulips are eaten.

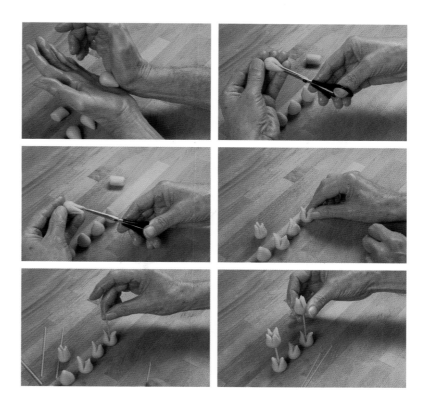

HEART

Roll out a standard stick and place this in the palm of your hand.

Gently flatten out the central section, and then carefully fold the two ends together. Smooth it into shape by pressing gently with both palms.

MODEL BASES

Melt chocolate in a basin sitting over a pan of barely simmering water. Stir in unsweetened puffed rice and, if you wish, ground nuts for more flavor.

Spoon onto a piece of baking parchment and flatten with a palette knife into small cookies or the required size.

Leave to set.

Molding tools

Molds and modeling tools.

Note: The marzipan figures in this book are both decorative and delicious to eat. However, when eating the figures, please remember the following:
• If toothpicks or dry spaghetti have been used as fixings, ensure that these have all been removed before eating the figures.
• Remove all non-edible accessories before eating.
• Food coloring may cause allergic reactions.
• Models using raw egg white as fixings should not be eaten by pregnant women, children, or the elderly.

Designs

Valentine's Day

Color a small amount of marzipan dark brown using instant coffee
granules or brown food coloring.

Mold the bears as described on page 17.

Using the dark brown marzipan, roll tiny balls to make their noses.

Attach these to the faces and use frosting for the eyes.

Use the point of a sharp knife to cut an open mouth.

Make two little marzipan balls for the ears and place them on the head.

Decorate with red fondant hearts.

Valentine's Day bears

Love serenade

◉

All the figures are made on a base of chocolate or marzipan in the shape of a cylinder.

Color the marzipan paste pink for the head and hands.

Next, color a sufficient amount of marzipan paste yellow for the singer's jacket.

Color some marzipan paste dark brown for the musicians' jackets.

Roll out smooth balls of pink marzipan for the heads, and attach smaller balls of pink marzipan to these for the nose, mouth, and ears.

Attach the heads to their chocolate or marzipan cylindrical bases.

Roll out the marzipan for each jacket.

Drape it around the cylinder, and create the arms and hands in the appropriate color.

Press two different sized balls of black marzipan flat and lay them on the singer's head, then make grooves with a knife to shape the hairstyle.

Decorate with frosting to make the eyes and the musicians' hair.

Finally, add the flower and the musical instruments to complete the scene.

Young love

Make a puffed-rice and chocolate base for each model (see page 24), and leave to set.

Color the marzipan for the hair as you wish, and color enough marzipan a deep red for the heart.

Create the couple as shown on page 17.

Squeeze the marzipan for the hair through a garlic press and attach to the head.

Use frosting to make the eyes.

Make the red marzipan heart as shown on page 24.

Place each model on its own base.

Woodland creatures

Color a little marzipan paste dark brown for the tails and ears.

Roll out a bulb shape as described on page 15.

Press down gently on it to flatten one side slightly and prevent it from rolling.

Model the tail and the ears, and attach them to the body.

Use the modeling tool to make the mouth shape and dip a toothpick in food coloring to mark the eyes.

Mice

Owls

Color a little of the marzipan paste yellow for the beak and brown for the eyebrows.

Use a smooth ball for the head and a larger, slightly flattened, oval one for the body.

Stick a toothpick through the body, and affix the head on top.

Use a modeling tool to press small hollows into the body, and then create the colored marzipan beaks and eyebrows.

Attach the beaks and eyebrows and add frosting for the eyes.

Note: The toothpick should be removed before eating.

Toadstool

Color a sufficient amount of marzipan paste red to make the toadstool's cap. Color a tiny amount of marzipan paste pink for the nose.

For the toadstool stalk, create a bulb shape and cut off the pointed end.

Press the cap onto the toadstool stalk, and finish off with coloring, frosting for the eyes and spots, and a small ball of pink marzipan for the nose.

For the body, color sufficient amounts of marzipan paste yellow and green.

Color the rest pink for the head.

Use the green marzipan to make the legs.

Use the yellow marzipan to make the upper body and the arms.

Attach the arms and legs to the body. Add feet made from sugared almonds (dragées) or candy-coated chocolate buttons.

Set aside a little pink marzipan for the nose and mouth. Roll the rest into a smooth ball and attach to the top of the body.

Model the nose and the mouth using little balls of pink marzipan, and add frosting for the eyes, frosting for the beard, the flower, and the hat.

Gnome

⊙

Rabbits

Color a little ball of marzipan paste brown using instant coffee granules.

Leave the rest in its natural color.

From one ball of marzipan, mold four limbs as shown on page 17.

Mold a pear shape for the head, bisecting the narrow end to create two ears.

Use a modeling tool to add more detail, then attach the head to the body.

Use frosting to make the rabbit's eyes, and cut a mouth shape using a

the modeling tool.

Use the brown marzipan to create a little ball for the nose and attach it to the face.

Make one large and three small rabbits in this way, and group them together.

Fox

{

Color a sufficient amount of marzipan paste pale yellow.
Color a smaller amount brown using instant coffee granules
or food coloring.
Mold the fox's body as described on page 17.
Mold a bulb shape for the head as described on page 21, and
use a pointed modeling tool to shape the ears.
Use the brown marzipan to make the fox's brush and whiskers
and a little ball for the nose and attach them to the model.
Dip the fox's feet in melted chocolate.

Moles

Color a sufficient amount of marzipan paste pink and orange for the bodies and brown for the limbs and noses.

Model pointed, pear-shaped balls for the bodies as described on page 15.

Gently press them into a lying or standing position on the work surface.

Model the limbs using the brown marzipan, and attach these to the bodies.

Roll out little balls for the noses and fix these to the bodies.

Use the point of a modeling tool to create the eyes.

Eggcup men

To make the eggcups, attach the two halves of a small chocolate Easter egg end-to-end using melted chocolate.

Color a small quantity of marzipan yellow for the hands and brown for the nose, and give the rest of it an eggshell color.

Use the eggshell-colored marzipan to roll out smooth ovals to the size and shape of an egg. Place them in the chocolate eggcups.

Use a paintbrush to speckle the eggs with tiny dots of food coloring.

Make a small ball of brown marzipan for the nose and place it on the face.

Create the eyes and finish with black and white frosting. Dip the end of a modeling tool in brown food coloring and form two grooves for the eyebrows. Now dip in red food coloring and form the mouth.

Mold the hand, attach it to the body using melted chocolate, then attach the spoon.

Decorate with sugar mini-eggs.

Easter

Easter treats

Chicken and rooster

Easter

Make two foot-shaped bases from yellow marzipan dipped in chocolate.

For the rooster, fix a white chocolate egg to the base in an upright position.

For the chicken, place a dark chocolate egg on its side on the other base.

Mold two balls of marzipan for the heads.

Color some marzipan yellow for the beaks, red for the combs, brown for the rooster's neck, and orange for the collars.

Lay a small roll of brown marzipan around the rooster's neck and attach a mini egg with melted chocolate.

Create two small orange marzipan bulb shapes (see page 15), and use sharp scissors to cut open the beaks.

Attach a beak to each head.

Roll out the red marzipan thinly and cut out the shapes of the combs. Attach them to the heads.

Roll out the orange marzipan for the collars, and cut them to shape using a knife.

Fix them to the eggs, and then press the heads into position on top.

Mold the wings for the chicken, and decorate with chocolate mini-eggs.

Ducklings

Make a patterned base from marzipan colored green and dipped
in chocolate on one side.
Color the rest of the marzipan paste yellow.
Use two-thirds of the yellow marzipan to mold a bulb shape, then position
it on the model base by resting it on its side and angling the pointed end
slightly upward.
Leave a small quantity apart for the little wings and mold the rest to form
the head: create a bulb shape, flatten out the pointed end for the beak,
and complete the expression using a knife.
Mold the wings, and attach the head and wings to the body.
Use frosting to make the eyes and orange food coloring to paint the beak.
Decorate the base with jelly beans.

Easter

Big *Easter bunny*

Easter

Create a model base (see page 24), place on it a large, pointed egg made of chocolate or marzipan, and leave to set.

Create a bulb shape for the head. Use scissors to make the ears, shaping the finished design with your fingers.

Make smooth little balls of marzipan for the nose and the mouth, and mold the hands. Attach them to the body with melted chocolate.

Color a little marzipan red and roll it out thinly to make a scarf to drape around the neck.

Finish by using frosting to make the eyes and decorating with food coloring and mini-eggs.

Cute animals

Piglets

Color the marzipan paste pink.

Create a body with four limbs as described on page 17.

Place the body in the position you want.

Mold a pear shape for the head, and flatten out the end as shown on page 20.

Use a sharp knife to make the incision for the mouth.

Make two little balls of marzipan for the ears, flatten these out between your thumb
and forefinger, and attach to either side of the head.

Make the eyes using black and white frosting, and prick out the nostrils using a toothpick or modeling tool.

Finish off the decoration with your choice of accessories, but make it clear if they are edible or inedible.

Dog with puppies

Color a sufficient amount of marzipan paste brown for the ears, noses, and mouths.

Mold one large and three small bodies as described on page 17.

Shape one large and three small heads, and attach them to the bodies.

Create the noses, ears, and mouths using the brown marzipan, attach them to the heads, and then use frosting to make the eyes.

◉

Create a pear shape as described on page 15.
Using the point of a knife, cut into the sides to make the wings, and gently
flatten the top of the head and pinch out a beak.
Dip the back half of the figure into melted chocolate and leave to set.
Use frosting to make the eyes and use orange food coloring to paint on the beak.

Penguins

Four bear cubs

with skis in the snow

Color a small amount of marzipan paste brown using instant coffee granules or food coloring.

Create four bodies (see page 17) and four heads.

Attach the heads to the bodies.

Roll out four little balls of brown marzipan for the noses.

Attach these to the heads, and use frosting to make the bear cubs' eyes.

Decorate with skis and ski poles.

Springtime

Color the marzipan paste various colors for the tulip flowers and green for the leaves.

To make the flowers, create a bulb shape (see page 23).

Cut crossways into the pointed end using sharp scissors, and then carefully open out the petals.

To make the leaves, use sharp scissors to cut just once into the green bulb.

Then fasten the leaves to a small block of marzipan using a piece of dry spaghetti 3 inches in length and painted with green food coloring.

Place the colored tulip flower on top.

Note: The spaghetti stem should be removed before eating.

Field of tulips

Ladybugs

Create smooth balls and cut these in half and flatten slightly.

Use the sharp edge of a knife to create the lines for the head and the wings.

Dip the head into melted chocolate.

Make small hollows in the wings.

Paint the wings red and add use frosting to make the eyes.

Finish with legs cut from thin black card.

Note: The card legs should be removed before eating.

A trip to the zoo

○

Color the marzipan for the noses brown. Color the rest of the paste orange.

For the mother, use orange marzipan to mold a body as shown on page 16, but mold its second limb into a tail shape.

Create the legs as described on page 24 for the heart, but without pressing them together. Make two small front legs and two large hind legs. Attach them to the body.

Mold the head as indicated on page 21, and attach to the body.

Make two small hearts for the baby kangaroo's legs, and model the head in the same way as for its mother. Attach it between its mother's legs.

Model the ears using orange marzipan and the noses using brown marzipan, attaching them to the head. Use a modeling tool to make the mouth and add detail to the paws. Finish off by using frosting to make the eyes.

Kangaroo

Hippos

Color the marzipan paste pink or orange and a small amount of
brown for the tails.

Create a smooth ball for the body of each animal.

Mold a blunt pear-shaped ball for the head.

Attach the head to the body.

Use little balls of marzipan to make the ears, and use a knife to cut
a mouth.

Use a modeling tool to create the nostrils and the raised eye sockets.

Finish off by using frosting to make the eyes.

To make the tail, roll a small ball of brown marzipan between your
thumb and index finger and place it on the body.

Elephants

Color the marzipan for the ears brown.

Create a body as described on page 17.

Create the head as described on page 22 and add brown marzipan ears.

Attach the head to the body.

Mark the trunk with a modeling tool.

Finish off by using frosting to make the eyes.

Wild boar

Color most of the marzipan orange and the remainder brown for the ears, tusks, and tail.
Create a pear shape as described on page 15.
Set the ball down and gently flatten it slightly against the work surface to prevent
it from rolling over.
Use the edge of your palms to press the marzipan upward to form a thin ridge, and cut
the spines with scissors or the point of a sharp knife.
Flatten the nose end, create nostrils with a modeling tool, and use a knife to cut a
mouth into the front.
Model the ears, tusks, and tail in brown marzipan, and attach these to the body.
Finish off by using frosting to make the eyes.

Swiss yodelers

All the figures are formed around a body made of chocolate or marzipan in the shape of an upended egg.

Place the wide end of the body on a circular base made of chocolate or card.

Color the marzipan paste for the head and hands pink.

Color the marzipan for the hair, jackets, and scarves separately.

Roll out smooth balls for the heads from half of the pink marzipan.

Create the ears, noses, and mouths and attach these to the heads.

Squeeze the marzipan for the hair through a garlic press, and style on the heads.

Place each head on a chocolate/marzipan body.

Roll out the marzipan for each jacket and scarf, draping these around the body.

Create the hands from pink marzipan and attach.

Use candy-coated chocolate buttons or sugared almonds (dragées) for the feet, and fix these to the base with a little melted chocolate.

Finish off with frosting for open eyes, or mark closed eyes with a modeling tool, and add a couple of toy hats.

Note: Remove hats and card bases before eating.

Geishas

These figures are molded around a cylinder-shaped body base made of chocolate or marzipan.

Place the cylinder on a circular chocolate or card base.

Color a third of the marzipan paste pink, using it to make a smooth ball for each head.

Color a third of the marzipan in the color you want for the kimono.

With the remainder, color a third for the hair, a third for the sleeves, and a third for the collar.

Attach the head to the chocolate/marzipan body.

Roll out a rectangle of marzipan for the kimono, round off the corners, and drape it
around the body base.

Squeeze the marzipan for the hair through a garlic press, and arrange on the head.

Roll out the marzipan for the sleeves, and attach around the top of the body.

Model the remaining details, and use candy-coated chocolate buttons or sugared almonds
(dragées) for the feet.

Finish off by using frosting to decorate the figures and make the eyes, and add dry spaghetti hair pins.

Note: Remove any inedible decorations and card bases before eating.

Soccer team

Color a sufficient amount of marzipan green and roll out to create an even rectangle for the soccer pitch.

The soccer players and the referee are molded around a cylinder-shaped body base made of chocolate or marzipan.

Attach the bodies to chocolate bases. Push green marzipan through a garlic press and model the grass round the feet on the chocolate bases.

Color the marzipan for the heads and hands pink.

Then color a sufficient amount of marzipan to make the players' shirts in the colors you want, and color the referee's shirt black.

Roll out smooth balls of pink marzipan for the heads, attaching a nose and ears to each one, and a mouth for about half the team, using smaller balls. Make a mouth with a modeling tool for the rest of the players and the referee.

Attach the heads to the chocolate/marzipan body.

Roll out the colored sheets of marzipan for the players' shirts and stack one on top of the other in alternate colors. Cut the stack into narrow strips. Drape a strip around each player and make arms in the matching colors.

Model the hands using the pink marzipan and attach.

Make a shirt for the referee, using the black marzipan, and make his hair. Make him some red and yellow cards.

Squeeze the marzipan for the players' hair through a garlic press, and apply the hair to the heads.

Use frosting to make the eyes.

Roll out small, smooth balls of marzipan, placing them at the players' feet. Mark them in soccer-ball style using a sharp knife or modeling tool.

The professor

The professor is created around a cylinder-shaped body base made from chocolate or
brown-colored marzipan.

Color the marzipan paste for the head and hands pink.

Roll out a smooth ball for the head and attach smaller balls of marzipan for the nose and ears.

Make an indent for the mouth with a modeling tool.

Fix the head to the chocolate/marzipan body.

Roll out white marzipan for the jacket, drape it around the body, and form the arms.

Model the hands using the pink marzipan and attach.

Model two "wings" of hair, fix them in place on either side of the head, and color them gray.

Finish off by using frosting to make the eyes.

Shape the computers from blocks of marzipan, completing the details with a modeling tool
or the point of a knife.

Color in the detail using a fine paintbrush and accessorize.

Color a sufficient amount of the marzipan paste pink to create the driver.

Next, color enough marzipan red for the racing car and blue for its wheels. Color a little for the hair or have fun making a small helmet instead. Roll out a smooth ball from the pink marzipan for the head and attach smaller balls for the nose, mouth, and ears.

Model the arms and hands from the remainder of the pink marzipan.

Make a thick roll from the blue marzipan and slice this into four pieces for the tires.

Use a modeling tool to create the circular grooves in the tires and the axle.

Roll out the red marzipan into an even stick shape; gently flatten at the front end of the racing car and model it into the desired design.

Use a spoon to make a smooth hollow in the middle of the car.

Use card to create the rear wing, and decorate the top with a strip of red marzipan.

Press the wheels onto the chassis, and place the driver in the hollow.

Note: The card should be removed before eating.

Formula 1 racing driver

Leisure time

The thin clown is formed around a cone-shaped chocolate body base, while the fatter figure is made
with two halves of a hollow chocolate egg stuck together with melted chocolate, and left to set.

Attach the clown figures to a chocolate base using melted chocolate.

Color some marzipan paste pink to make a hand and the clowns' heads.

Color some marzipan red for the jacket and bowtie of one of the clowns and green for the other.

Roll out the marzipan for the jackets and cut to shape.

Drape around the body bases.

From the pink marzipan, make two smooth balls for the heads and six smaller ones for the ears and noses.

Attach the ears and noses to the heads, then fix the heads to the body bases.

Mold the thinner clown's hand from pink marzipan and attach. Add accessories of your choice.

Create bowties from the remainder of the colored marzipan and attach to the figures.

Add feet, if you wish, from candy-coated chocolate buttons.

Create the eyes and mouths using the point of a knife, and top the figures with little paper hats.

Note: Remove non-edible accessories before eating.

Clowns

Create three bodies as described on page 17.

Color a small amount of marzipan paste brown for the elephant's ears and for the noses of the other two figures.

For their hats, color small amounts of the marzipan blue, yellow, and green.

Create the elephant's head as described on page 22.

Use some brown marzipan to make the elephant's ears.

Create the dog's head as described on page 19 and the cat's head as described on page 21.

Make noses from the remainder of the brown marzipan, and attach them to the heads of the dog and cat. Indent the mouths with a modeling tool.

Place the heads on the bodies.

Make the hats and place these on the heads.

Finally, use frosting to make the eyes.

Circus animals

Diver with sea creatures

Color some marzipan paste pink for the head and hands.

Color a small amount of marzipan paste yellow for the diver's mask and belt.

Color the rest dark blue.

Use a flat piece of wood to roll out an even stick of marzipan.

Use scissors to bisect each end and create a prone figure.

Use your fingers to model the flippers and the arm movements.

Create the hands and the head, and attach these to the body.

Create the diver's mask and belt using the yellow marzipan, and attach these around the figure's head and waist.

Use frosting to make the eyes and to decorate the mask and belt, and add cellophane to represent the glass of the mask.

Shape the marzipan sea creatures in molds and use coloring to decorate them.

Note: Remove cellophane before eating.

Beach huts

Color sufficient amounts of marzipan paste blue and red for the huts and brown for their roofs.
Roll out even sheets of blue, red, and uncolored marzipan.
Stack them alternately one on top of the other and gently press together.
Use a sharp knife to cut out blocks from the stack, incorporating a peaked roof shape.
Roll out the brown marzipan and use a sharp knife to cut out the roofing. Attach to the beach huts.
Use the point of a sharp knife to create the door.

Sunbathers

Reserve a little uncolored marzipan for the bikini top.
Color some marzipan paste pink for the body and yellow for the hair.
Use two-thirds of the pink marzipan to create a body and place it in a toy deckchair.
Create two smaller-sized balls for the bust and fix these in position.
Create a smooth ball for the head, and attach this to the body. Mark the features using a modeling tool.
Squeeze the yellow marzipan through a garlic press and arrange on the head.
Roll out a thin layer of natural colored marzipan and use it to make the bikini top. Attach this over the figure's bust.
Use the same method for the child as for the sunbather but without the deckchair and bust.

New Year's visitor

Make a puffed-rice and chocolate base (see page 24), and leave to set.

The figure is formed around a cone-shaped chocolate body base.

Color some marzipan paste brown for the jacket and the arms.

with champagne

Color a little of the marzipan pink for the hands.

Roll out a large, smooth ball of marzipan for the head and attach smaller balls for the nose and cheeks.

Attach the head to the body base.

Roll out the marzipan for the jacket, drape it around the upper body, and add brown marzipan arms with pink marzipan hands.

Make a scarf from white marzipan and drape it round the neck.

Finish off the face by using frosting to make the eyes and red food coloring to paint the mouth and cheeks.

Complete the figure with a hat, cane, candy feet, and champagne bottle.

Note: Remove inedible accessories before eating.

The figure is formed around a cone-shaped chocolate body base attached
to a chocolate base.
Color a sufficient amount of marzipan paste red for the arms, jacket, and hat.
Roll out a smooth ball of marzipan for the head, then attach smaller balls
for the nose and cheeks.
Attach the head to the body base.
Roll out the marzipan for the jacket and hat, drape around the body, and
create the arms from the remaining red marzipan.
Use frosting to make the eyes and beard, and complete the facial features
using food coloring. Trim the hat with frosting and place a little gift
wrapped box in the arms of the figure.
Note: Remove inedible accessories before eating.

Santa Claus

Candles

Make a puffed-rice and chocolate base (see page 24), and leave to set.

Model the candle by twisting a block of marzipan, and attaching it to the base.

Use a toasted almond for the flame, and finish decorating with frosting and coloring and a couple of little gift wrapped boxes.

Heavenly choir

Color a sufficient amount of marzipan paste pink for the heads and yellow for the hair.

Roll out four bulb shapes for the bodies, flattening the base to keep them standing upright.

Roll out the marzipan for the cloaks and cut out four ovals. Drape the cloaks around the bodies.

Roll out four smooth balls of marzipan for the heads and add smaller balls for the mouths and noses.

Make the hands and attach them to the cloaks.

Model the hair from rolled-out yellow marzipan, and attach to the head.

Use frosting to make angels with open eyes or fashion closed lids with a modeling tool.

four singing angels

Mother's Day

Make a puffed-rice and chocolate base (see page 24), and leave to set.

Stick the two halves of a hollow chocolate drop or egg together with melted chocolate.

Attach it to the base and leave to set.

Color one third of the marzipan paste green.

Divide the remaining marzipan into three, and make each piece a different color.

Roll out the marzipan and cut out leaves and flowers with a sharp knife.

Fix them together using a little melted chocolate, and then attach the completed flower to the chocolate egg.

Decorate with candy-coated chocolate buttons.

Color a sufficient amount of marzipan paste pink for the head and the hands.

Color a sufficient amount of marzipan paste brown for the legs and red or green for the body.

Use the brown marzipan to create the lower half of the body and a pair of legs.

Use the red or green marzipan to create the upper half of the body and a pair of arms, and press the two halves together.

Balance the figure securely around the neck of a bottle.

Create the head and hands from the pink marzipan and attach to the body.

Complete the face with pink marzipan ears, mouth and nose. Use frosting to make the eyes, or mark closed eyelids and mouth with a modeling tool.

Squeeze yellow marzipan through a garlic press and model the hair, or use white frosting.

Make a hat from a flattened ball of black marzipan attached to a thin flat circle of black marzipan. Attach to the top of the head.

Create the feet using two sugared almonds (dragées) or candy-coated chocolate buttons.

Father's Day

Reptiles and Dinosaurs

Lizard

Make a puffed-rice and chocolate base (see page 24), and leave to set.

Color a sufficient amount of marzipan paste pale blue.

Color a little of the marzipan brown for the legs, horn, and nose and pink for the ears.

Use the blue marzipan to roll out a stick, forming a point at one end for the tail.

Using both hands, gently flatten out the stick slightly.

Using a pair of sharp scissors, snip spikes along the reptile's back and tail, leaving the head end smooth, and attach the body to the base.

Make the legs using most of the brown marzipan. Attach them to the body.

Roll out two small balls of pink marzipan, gently flatten them between your thumb and forefinger, and attach to the head.

With the remaining brown marzipan, make a small horn and a little ball for the nose and attach both to the head. Make a second horn with yellow marzipan.

Use a modeling tool dipped in black food coloring to form the eyes and mouth, and paint a little pink color along the spikes.

Brontosaurus

Make a puffed-rice and chocolate base (see page 24), and leave to set.

Color a sufficient amount of marzipan paste light brown.

Create a body as shown on page 16, extending one end of the body into a tail and the other into a neck and head.

Mold the hind legs and forelegs, and attach them to the body.

Balance the figure securely on the base.

Use a knife to cut the open mouth, and finish off by using frosting to make the eyes.

Make a little nose from brown marzipan and a tongue from red marzipan and attach both to the face.

Lightly paint green food coloring onto the underbelly.

Stegosaurus

◉

Make a puffed-rice and chocolate base (see page 24), and leave to set.

Color a sufficient amount of marzipan paste mauve.

Color a little marzipan yellow for the spines.

Create a body as shown on page 16, extending one end of the body into a tail
and the other into a neck and head.

Create the hind legs and forelegs, and attach to the body.

Balance the figure securely on the base.

Use a knife to cut the open mouth, and finish off by using frosting to make the eyes.

Roll out the yellow marzipan into a long, flat strip, cut into spikes with a sharp knife,
and attach to the back.

Alligator

Make a puffed-rice and chocolate base (see page 24), and leave to set.

Color a sufficient amount of marzipan paste yellow and red for the tulips.

Color the rest of the marzipan green.

Create bulb shapes from the yellow and red marzipan for the flowers, and model as described on page 23.

Create two bulb shapes for the leaves using some of the green marzipan, and attach to the base.

Fix the flowers on top of toothpicks painted with green food coloring, then push the toothpicks between the leaves.

Roll out a long stick of marzipan for the alligator's body, and push out both ends into a point.

Create two front legs and attach them to the body.

Place the figure in a standing position on the base, bending the tail to lie flat and help support the alligator.

Gently push the point of the head into a horizontal position, and use scissors to cut open the mouth. Push a small piece of red marzipan into the mouth for the tongue.

Use small balls of marzipan to create the nose and raised eye sockets.

Finish off with frosting to make the eyes.

Note: Take care when using toothpicks as they are very sharp—make sure they are removed before eating.

Frog

Color a sufficient amount of marzipan green for the body, create an oval ball, and cut this in half. Next, take the same quantity of white marzipan, create another oval ball, and cut this in half as well.

Place one half of the green ball on top of one half of the white ball, then use a modeling tool to mold this into the shape of the frog's body.

Take some green marzipan for the feet and roll out a long stick. Fold the ends toward each other and shape them into webbed feet using a modeling tool.

Firmly attach the body to the feet.

Separate the green and white marzipan segments slightly to form an open mouth.

Make a tongue from bright red marzipan and fix it in the mouth.

Finish off by using frosting to make the eyes and add a little gold crown.

Ghosts

You could work with pastillage (a sugar-based dough) to create a pure white ghost, but you can also make a lovely ghost simply by using white marzipan. You can buy pastillage ready-made from specialty stores.

The figures are molded around a cone-shaped marzipan body base with a small, smooth ball of marzipan on top for the head. Stick a toothpick through the head and into the body to secure the marzipan ball firmly.

Roll out the pastillage or marzipan to a 1/4-inch thickness.

Cut around a circular mold with a sharp knife to create circles, and drape these around the body base to form folds.

Use a pointed modeling tool dipped in black food coloring to prick out the eyes and a mouth.

Decorate with spiders or other spooky items.

Note: Take care when using toothpicks as they are very sharp—make sure the toothpicks and inedible accessories are removed before eating.

Pumpkin heads

Color a sufficient amount of marzipan paste yellow for the heads, brown for the
five bodies and one of the cloaks, green for three more cloaks, and black for the
final cloak. You will also need some white marzipan for the final cloak.
Color a little marzipan pink for the hands, and color a small piece red for the noses.
Roll out five bulb shapes from the brown marzipan to make the bodies, pressing the
base flat to keep them standing upright.
Roll out a piece from the remaining brown marzipan and cut out an oval to make a
cloak. Drape it around one of the bodies.
Repeat using the green marzipan, cutting out three ovals and draping them around
another three bodies. Make a black-and-white cloak for the last body.
Using the yellow marzipan, roll out five smooth balls for the heads, creating the
typical pumpkin grooves with a modeling tool.
Model some pumpkin stalks and fix these to the top of the heads.
Color the stalks using a little green coloring and a fine paintbrush.
Roll out the red marzipan into little balls for noses and attach these to the faces.
Finish off by using frosting to make the eyes and use a modeling tool dipped in
black food coloring to make the mouths.
Create the hands from pink marzipan, and attach to the bodies.
If you want to add feet, use candy-coated chocolate buttons.
Roll out yellow balls of marzipan for the pumpkins, flatten them slightly,
and make grooves using a modeling tool as before.
Model pumpkin stalks, attach and color as before.

Witch and wizard

Color a sufficient amount of marzipan paste dark brown or black for a body, cloak, and the wizard's hair, light brown for the other body and a second cloak, and pink for the heads and the hands.

Color some marzipan yellow to make the witch's hair and the pumpkins.

Create a bulb shape using the dark brown marzipan and another using the light brown marzipan.

Roll out the marzipan into an oval for the cloaks, and drape them around the bodies.

Use the pink marzipan to create two smooth balls for the heads, and model a long chin on each.

Roll out little balls of pink marzipan for the noses and the warts, and attach these to the faces.

Color the noses and warts using a fine paintbrush and suitable coloring.

Create the hands and attach to the figures.

Squeeze yellow and dark brown or black marzipan through a garlic press and model the figures' hair.

To make the hats, model the marzipan into a a cone shape, roll out a disk to form the brim, and place securely on the figures' heads.

Finish off the faces using a modeling tool and frosting.

Roll out yellow balls of marzipan for the pumpkins, flatten them slightly, and make grooves in the sides using a modeling tool.

Make a long, thin stick of marzipan for the pumpkin stalks. Cut into short segments, and attach to the pumpkins. Color the stalks using a paintbrush and a little green food coloring.

Decorate with suitable accessories.

Note: Remove any inedible accessories before eating.

DESIGNS AND RECIPES
Guido Jans

EDITING AND STYLING
Véronique De Meyer

PHOTOGRAPHY
Michel De Meyer

GRAPHIC DESIGN
quod. voor de vorm.

TRANSLATION
JMS Books llp

Fall River Press
122 Fifth Avenue
New York, NY 10011

ISBN: 978-1-4351-1842-3

Printed and bound in China

1 3 5 7 9 10 8 6 4 2